MY FIRST BOOK OF
DINOSAURS

Katie Woolley

ARCTURUS

ARCTURUS

This edition published in 2016 by Arcturus Publishing Limited
26/27 Bickels Yard, 151–153 Bermondsey Street,
London SE1 3HA

Author: Katie Woolley
Designer: Neal Cobourne
Editor: Joe Harris

Picture credits:
Cover illustrations: Shutterstock. All other images: Arcturus Image Library (Stefano
Azzalin, Martin Bustamante, Juan Calle and Liberum Donum, Mat Edwards, Colin
Howard, Kunal Kundu, Jerry Pyke, Val Walerczuk); and Shutterstock.

ISBN 978-1-78599-268-1
CH004928NT
Supplier: 26, Date 0916, Print run 4670

Printed in China

CONTENTS

1. WHAT ARE DINOSAURS?

Dinosaurs were reptiles that walked the Earth for 165 million years, long before there were any humans. We know of about 700 types of dinosaurs. But scientists think there were at least 1,500.

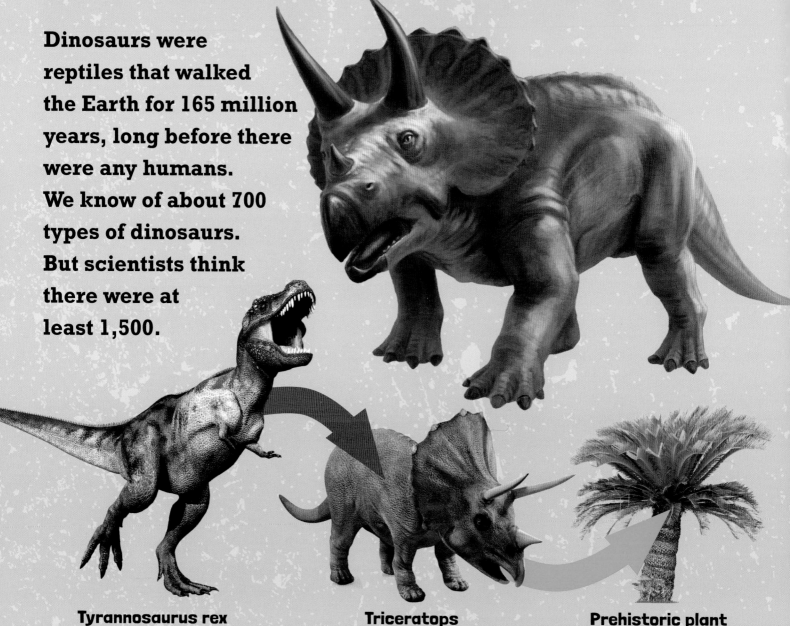

Tyrannosaurus rex

Triceratops

Prehistoric plant

Dinosaurs such as Triceratops (try-SEH-rah-tops) ate plants. The plant-eaters were hunted and eaten by meat-eaters such as Tyrannosaurus rex (ty-RAH-noh-sore-us rex).

Huayangosaurus
(hoy-YAN-goh-SORE-us)

Fast Facts

The scientist Richard Owen first used the word "dinosaur" in 1842. This was over 170 years ago!

Huayangosaurus' plates protected it from meat-eaters.

Dinosaur means "terrible lizard."

When did dinosaurs live?

Dinosaurs lived during three different periods. They first appeared during the Triassic (try-AH-sik). Next came the Jurassic (juh-RAH-sik). At the end of the Cretaceous (kreh-TAY-shuss), all the dinosaurs disappeared.

T. rex lived during the Cretaceous period.

In the Triassic period, dinosaurs lived on one giant continent called Pangaea (pan-JEE-uh). During the Jurassic period, Pangaea split apart. By the end of the Cretaceous period, it had broken into seven continents. There are still seven today.

Triassic period:
248 to 206 million years ago

Jurassic period:
206 to 144 million years ago

Cretaceous period:
144 to 65 million years ago

Humans only appeared 200,000 years ago!

The Cretaceous period saw the largest variety of dinosaurs. Each continent had its own species. During this period, the first flowers bloomed. Cretaceous dinosaurs, such as T. rex and Therizinosaurus (THEH-rih-ZIH-noh-SORE-us), were on top of the world … for now!

T. rex

Therizinosaurus

Fast Facts

Therizinosaurus' arms were 2.5 m (8 ft) long! T. rex's arms were only 1 m (3 ft) long.

All shapes and sizes

There were many types of dinosaur. Some walked on four legs. Others walked on two. Some were so tall, they could feed from the tops of tall trees. Others were small enough to hide among the ferns on the forest floor.

Argentinosaurus (AR-jen-TEE-noh-SORE-us) was the length of four buses. But Microraptor (MY-krow-rap-tor) was only the size of a crow!

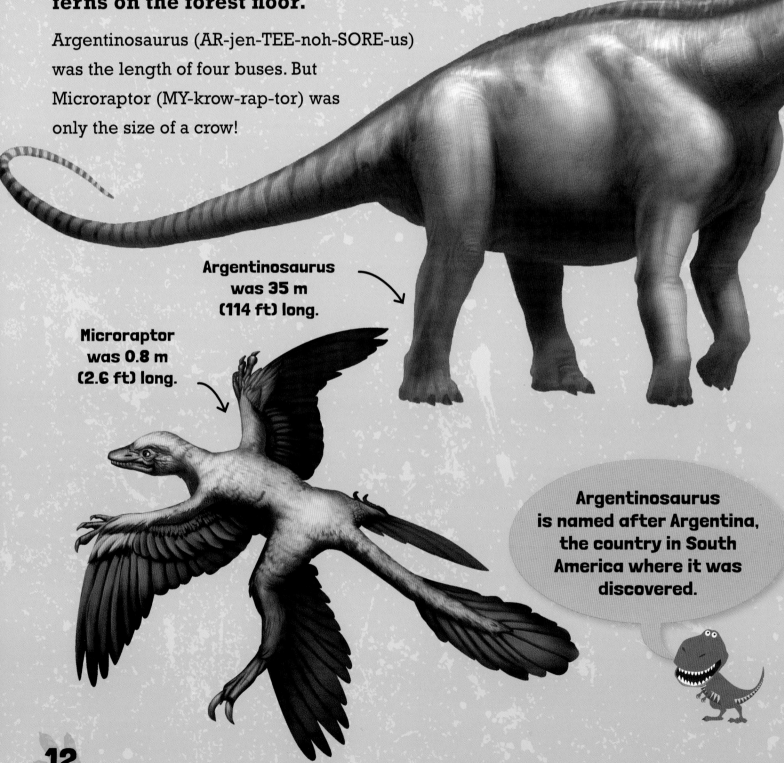

Argentinosaurus was 35 m (114 ft) long.

Microraptor was 0.8 m (2.6 ft) long.

Argentinosaurus is named after Argentina, the country in South America where it was discovered.

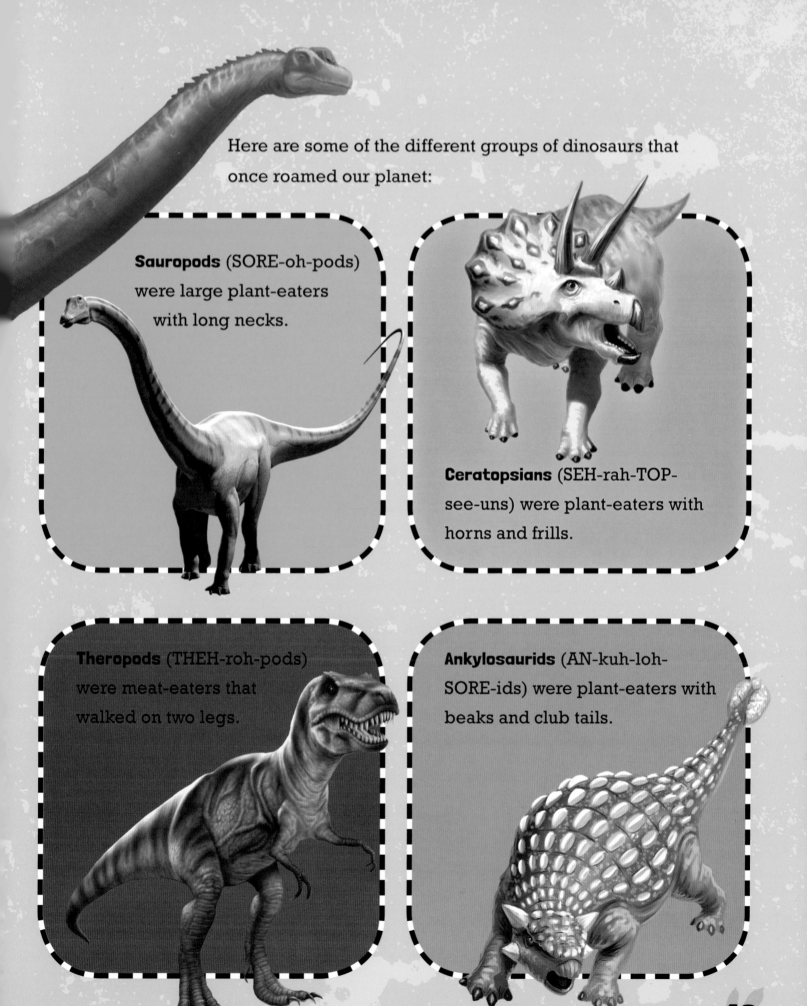

Here are some of the different groups of dinosaurs that once roamed our planet:

Sauropods (SORE-oh-pods) were large plant-eaters with long necks.

Ceratopsians (SEH-rah-TOP-see-uns) were plant-eaters with horns and frills.

Theropods (THEH-roh-pods) were meat-eaters that walked on two legs.

Ankylosaurids (AN-kuh-loh-SORE-ids) were plant-eaters with beaks and club tails.

13

High in the skies

Dinosaurs shared their world with other creatures, too. Pterosaurs (TEH-roh-sores) were winged reptiles that soared high in the sky. These animals ate sea creatures and insects. They also fed on dead animals, like vultures do today.

When on the ground, pterosaurs walked on all fours. They used the fingers on the end of their wings to balance.

Fast Facts

Pterosaurs had excellent eyesight. They could spot prey on the ground, far below!

Pterodactylus
(TEH-roh-DAK-till-us)

14

Tiny Nemicolopterus (NEH-mih-koh-LOP-teh-rus) was the size of a sparrow. The biggest pterosaur was Quetzalcoatlus (QWET-zul-koh-AT-lus). Its wingspan was 11 m (36 ft) wide. That's the same as a Spitfire, a type of old-fashioned plane.

Nemicolopterus

Quetzalcoatlus

Pterosaur means "winged lizard."

Under the sea

No dinosaurs lived in the ocean. However, there were many marine (water-dwelling) reptiles in prehistoric times. Plesiosaurs (PLEH-see-oh-SORES) had long necks and flippers. They moved quickly through the water.

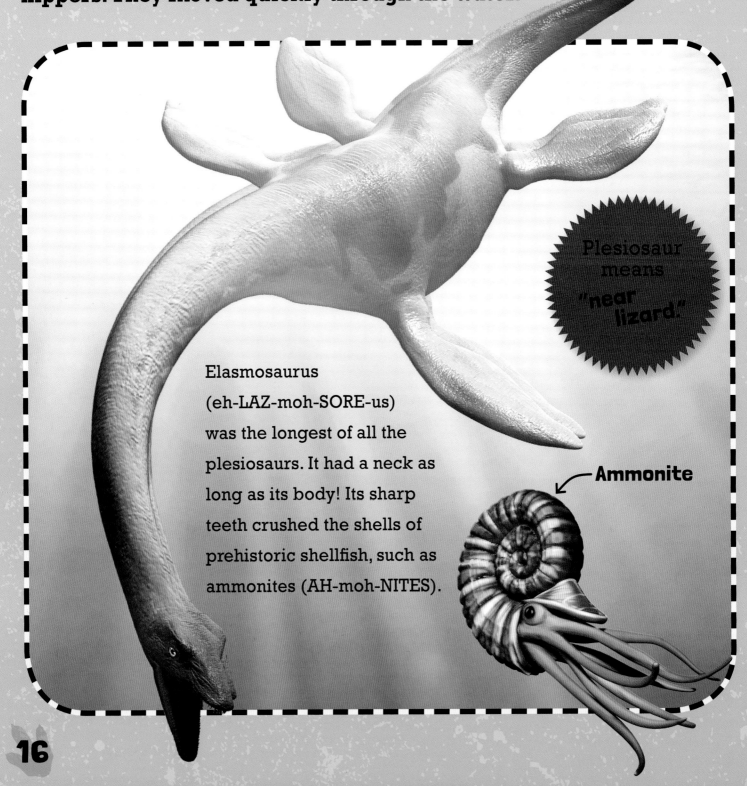

Plesiosaur means "near lizard."

Elasmosaurus (eh-LAZ-moh-SORE-us) was the longest of all the plesiosaurs. It had a neck as long as its body! Its sharp teeth crushed the shells of prehistoric shellfish, such as ammonites (AH-moh-NITES).

← Ammonite

Fast Facts

Marine reptiles had to come to the surface to breathe air, like today's whales and dolphins.

Shonisaurus
(SHOH-nee-SORE-us)

Shonisaurus was about five times bigger than a dolphin. It was 15 m (49 ft) long!

Were dinosaurs loving parents?

Most dinosaurs laid eggs, just like reptiles and birds do today. Dinosaur eggs came in all shapes and sizes, like the dinosaurs that laid them!

Most dinosaur eggs were oval or potato-shaped, but sauropod eggs were round. Some dinosaur eggs could fit in the palm of your hand. However, others were the size of a bowling ball!

A T. rex baby hatches from an egg.

T. rex nest

Adult T. rex

Triceratops young hatch from their eggs in the nest.

Some eggs were laid in mud and left to hatch. Other dinosaurs, such as Maiasaura (MY-ah-SORE-ah), may have looked after their eggs and babies until they were old enough to leave the nest.

Maiasaura means "good mother reptile."

Maiasaura

Record-breaking dinos

Which dinosaurs were the smartest, the heaviest, the tallest, and the lightest? Which had the biggest claws? Read on to find out ...

Scientists think that Troodon (TROH-oh-don) was the smartest dinosaur. For its body size, its brain was bigger than any other dinosaur.

The heaviest dinosaur is Brachiosaurus. It weighed 80 tonnes (88 tons)—that's the same as 17 elephants!

The dinosaur with the longest claws was Therizinosaurus. Its enormous claws were almost 1 m (3.3 ft) long!

The smallest and lightest dinosaur we know of is Microraptor. It weighed 1.8 kilograms (4 pounds). That's lighter than a chihuahua!

The tallest dinosaur of all was called Sauroposeidon (SORE-oh-poh-SIGH-don). It was 18.5 m (60 ft) tall. That's as tall as three giraffes!

What happened to the dinosaurs?

Nobody really knows why the dinosaurs vanished about 65 million years ago. During this mass extinction, dinosaurs, pterosaurs, and many marine reptiles were killed.

Most scientists think that a huge meteorite hit Earth. This sent a cloud of dust into the sky that blocked out light and heat from the Sun.

Fast Facts

In the 1990s, scientists discovered a crater 180 km (112 miles) wide in Mexico. Could it have been caused by a meteorite hitting Earth 65 million years ago?

Some scientists think that volcanoes also played a part in the extinction of the dinosaurs. Ash from volcanoes could have also blocked the Sun's heat and light. Either of these disasters would have made the weather very cold. Could this have wiped out the dinosaurs?

How do we know about dinosaurs?

We can find out about prehistoric times by looking at fossils. Fossils are the remains of living things that have been buried under mud or sand for millions of years. They have slowly turned to rock.

It takes a long time for scientists to uncover a fossil. They use special hammers and drills to carefully chip the rock away. Then the fossil is taken to a museum.

Fast Facts

A scientist who studies prehistoric fossils is called a paleontologist (PAY-lee-on-TOH-low-jist)

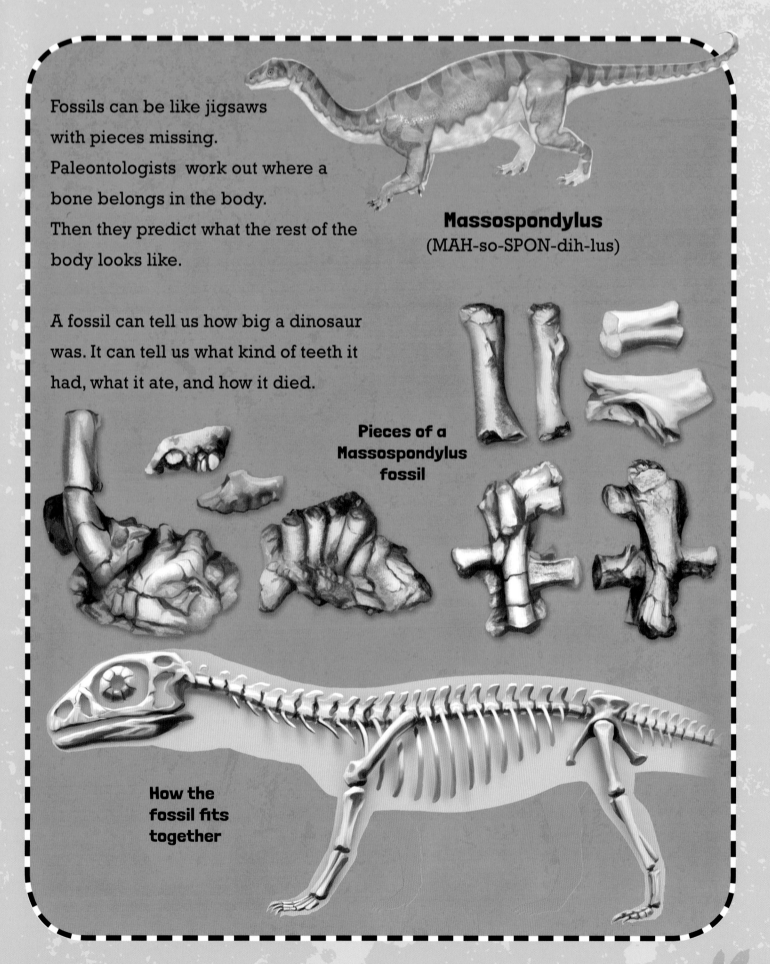

Fossils can be like jigsaws with pieces missing. Paleontologists work out where a bone belongs in the body. Then they predict what the rest of the body looks like.

A fossil can tell us how big a dinosaur was. It can tell us what kind of teeth it had, what it ate, and how it died.

Massospondylus
(MAH-so-SPON-dih-lus)

Pieces of a Massospondylus fossil

How the fossil fits together

Fossils around the world

Parasaurolophus

Diplodocus

Triceratops

Stegosaurus

Saltasaurus

Tyrannosaurus rex

Giganotosaurus

Dinosaur fossils have been found all over the world. Can you see any dinosaurs on this map that were found near where you live?

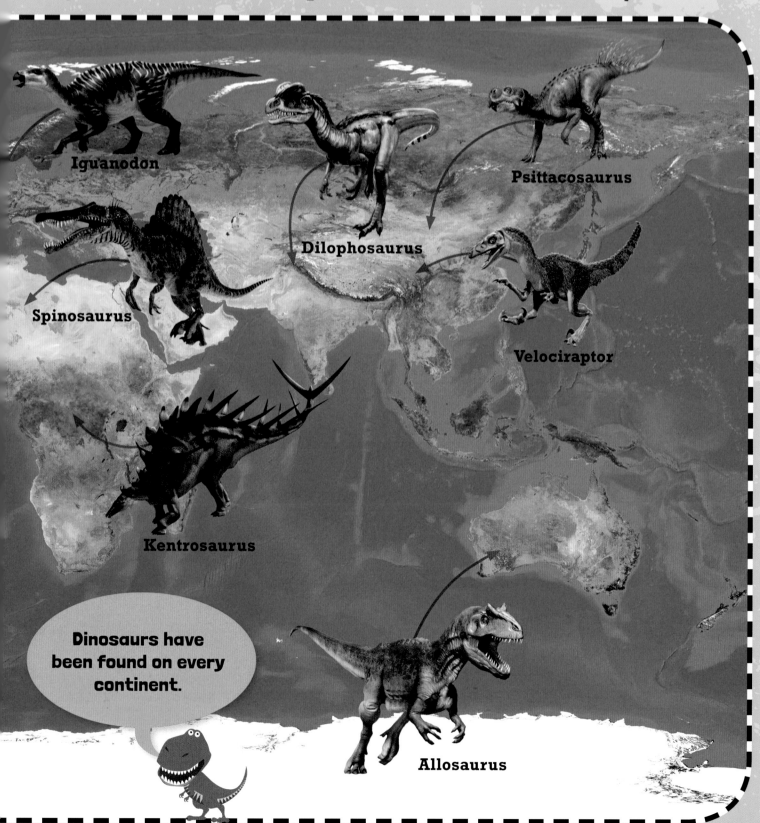

Iguanodon

Psittacosaurus

Dilophosaurus

Spinosaurus

Velociraptor

Kentrosaurus

Dinosaurs have been found on every continent.

Allosaurus

Dinosaurs and the world today

Some living creatures have barely changed since the time of the dinosaurs. Modern crocodiles, sharks, and scorpions are very similar to their prehistoric ancestors.

Modern birds are the descendants of dinosaurs. It's easy to see this from looking at a dinosaur like Caudipteryx (kaw-DIP-tuh-rix). This theropod was the size of a turkey, with a beak-like snout. It may have had feathers to keep warm, just like modern birds do.

Caudipteryx

The best place to discover dinosaurs is at your local natural history museum. There, you might be able to look at real dinosaur fossils!

"Natural history" is the science of animals and plants.

2. MIGHTY MEAT-EATERS

Meat-eating dinosaurs—the carnivores—were fast-moving, deadly hunters. They had razor-sharp teeth, strong back legs, and hooked claws on the ends of their toes.

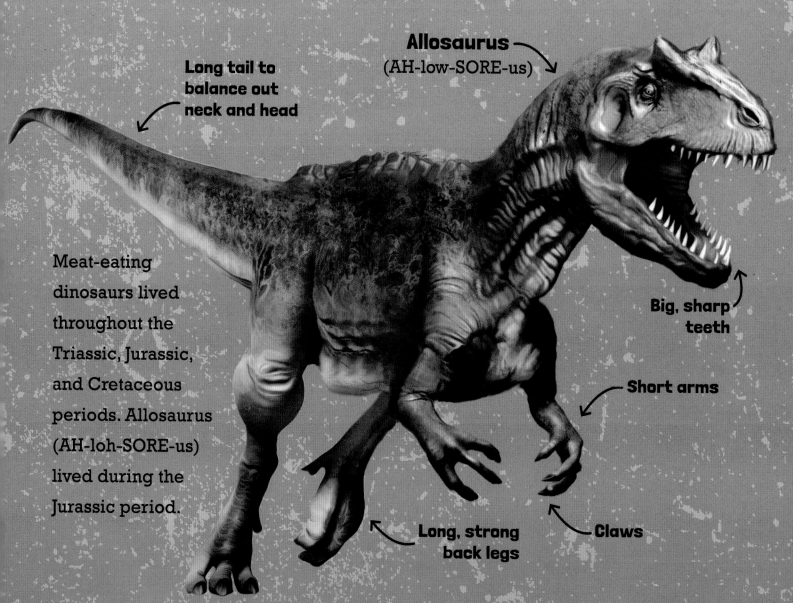

Allosaurus
(AH-low-SORE-us)

Long tail to
balance out
neck and head

Big, sharp
teeth

Short arms

Claws

Long, strong
back legs

Meat-eating dinosaurs lived throughout the Triassic, Jurassic, and Cretaceous periods. Allosaurus (AH-loh-SORE-us) lived during the Jurassic period.

Acrocanthosaurus (ah-crow-CAN-thoh-SORE-us) was a meat-eater with spines growing out of its back. It lived during the early Cretaceous period.

Most theropods walked on two legs. Theropod means **"beast-footed."**

Fast Facts

Most meat-eating dinosaurs were theropods (THEH-roh-pods). Some, such as Allosaurus and Acrocanthosaurus, were huge. Others were tiny.

Acrocanthosaurus

Sharp teeth

Fossilized teeth can help us learn more about dinosaurs. The teeth of a Tyrannosaurus rex were about 23 cm (9 inches) long. That's as long as a banana!

Some meat-eating dinosaurs were hunters, while some were scavengers, like modern hyenas. T. rex may have been both!

Fast Facts

The first dinosaurs were carnivores. Plant-eaters arrived later!

Meat-eating dinosaurs' powerful jaws snapped shut like a crocodile's. Their pointed teeth could pierce flesh and crush bones of bigger prey, such as Stegosaurus (STEH-goh-SORE-us). Some meat-eaters had serrated (saw-like) teeth that could rip off chunks of flesh and bone as they ate.

A theropod skull

A theropod feasting on its prey.

The thorny lizard

The largest meat-eating dinosaur was Spinosaurus (SPINE-oh-SORE-us). It was the length of two buses. The spines on its back were covered in skin, and looked like a sail. Each spine measured up to 2 m (6.5 ft) high—that's taller than most adults!

The "sail" might have been used to scare enemies or to attract a mate. It could have been used to cool the dinosaur down, too. Spinosaurus was possibly the first swimming dinosaur. It spent much of its life in water.

Spinosaurus weighed up to 18 tonnes (20 tons)—as much as 3 elephants!

Spinosaurus means "thorn lizard."

Fast Facts

When: Late Cretaceous period

Food: Other dinosaurs and large fish

Size: 18 m (59 ft) long

You!

Weight: 4,000 kg (4.4 tons)

How it moved: On two legs

Found in: Egypt and Morocco, Africa

Spinosaurus lived during the Cretaceous period, roaming the swamps of North Africa. It may have eaten dinosaurs, such as sauropods, as well as sharks and other large fish.

A tiny hunter

Hesperonychus (hes-puh-ruh-NIE-kus) was one of the smallest meat-eating dinosaurs that ever lived in North America. It was about the size of a pet cat. It was a deadly predator, although its prey was much smaller than T. rex's!

This tiny meat-eater ran on two legs and had an enlarged claw on its second toe. It probably hunted for food such as insects and small mammals. Forests and marshes were its hunting grounds.

Hesperonychus means "western claw."

Fast Facts

When: Late Cretaceous period

Food: Probably insects and small mammals

Size: About 60 cm (24 in) long

You!

Weight: 1.9 kg (4 lb)

How it moved: On two legs

Found in: North America

Hesperonychus weighed about as much as a chicken.

Hesperonychus may have had feathered wings that helped it glide from tree to tree. This way, it avoided larger predators on the ground.

Lone hunters or pack killers?

Some meat-eating dinosaurs hunted on their own, like tigers and bears. Others hunted in a pack, like wolves. We know this from fossils that show them living alone or in groups.

Yangchuanosaurus (yang-choo-AN-oh-SORE-us) was 10 m (32 ft) long—that's the length of two cars. But it may still have stalked its prey in packs.

Pack hunting would have made it easier to overcome larger prey, such as Mamenchisaurus (MAH-men-kee-SORE-us).

Yangchuanosaurus

Mamenchisaurus

Fast Facts

Some meat-eaters may have had saliva full of deadly bacteria. One bite could have poisoned and killed a victim!

Eoraptor (EE-oh-rap-tor) was one of the earliest pack-hunters. It had large eyes to see prey from far away.

Eoraptors

Fish for supper?

Suchomimus (SOO-koh-mim-us) was a large dinosaur with a body that was adapted for eating fish. Its long snout and huge claws were perfect for catching its slippery prey.

Suchomimus

Fast Facts

When: Early Cretaceous period

Food: Fish

Size: 10 m (33 ft) long

You!

Weight: 2,000 kg (2.2 tons)

How it moved: On two legs

Found in: The United Kingdom and Spain, Europe

Baryonyx (bah-ree-ON-icks) was a fish-eating dinosaur with a jaw like a crocodile's. It probably waded in water, waiting for its supper to swim by. Then it would use its large thumb claw like a hook, to stab a passing fish.

Baryonyx's teeth had a jagged edge, like a saw. They were curved inward, making it very hard for a fish to escape!

Baryonyx

Baryonyx means "heavy claw."

Suchomimus and Baryonyx were related to Spinosaurus.

Small but deadly

Aggressive, light, small, and speedy, Velociraptor (veh-LOH-see-rap-tor) was a ferocious predator. It was armed with sharp teeth and claws like daggers. A pack of these hunters could easily catch its prey.

Fast Facts

When: Late Cretaceous period

Food: Other animals

Size: 1.8 m (6 ft) long

← You!

Weight: 7–15 kg (15–33 lb)

How it moved: On two legs

Found in: Mongolia, Asia

Velociraptor was the size of a large dog and had strong back legs. It could run at up to 64 kilometers (40 miles) per hour. This meat-eater had 80 teeth and arms with three-fingered claws. A fearsome sight!

Velociraptor means "quick plunderer."

Velociraptor lived during the Cretaceous period.

In 1971, a fossil of Velociraptor and Protoceratops (pro-toe-SEH-rah-tops) locked in combat was found. Protoceratops was biting at the arm of the deadly predator, while Velociraptor attacked with its claws.

Protoceratops

Velociraptor

Giant southern reptile

Giganotosaurus (jee-gah-NOH-toh-sore-us) was BIG! This massive meat-eater lived 30 million years before T. rex came along, and was taller and heavier than its more famous cousin. Its teeth were as long as 20 cm (8 in)—bigger than an adult's hand.

At 12.5 m (41 ft) long, Giganotosaurus was about the size of a bus. But its brain was only about the size of a banana!

Giganotosaurus means "giant southern lizard."

Fast Facts

When: Early Cretaceous period

Food: Other animals

Size: 12.5 m (41 ft) long

You!

Weight: 4,000 kg (4.4 tons)

How it moved: On two legs

Found in: Argentina, South America

A complete fossil of this dinosaur has never been found. But scientists think Giganotosaurus ate large plant-eating dinosaurs, such as Argentinosaurus.

Giganotosaurus' sharp teeth had saw-like edges.

Argentinosaurus

Nest builder

Oviraptor (OH-vee-RAP-tor) was a bird-like dinosaur covered with feathers. Its toothless beak and curved jaws crushed its food. It had a small crest like a horn on its snout. The crest may have been used for mating displays.

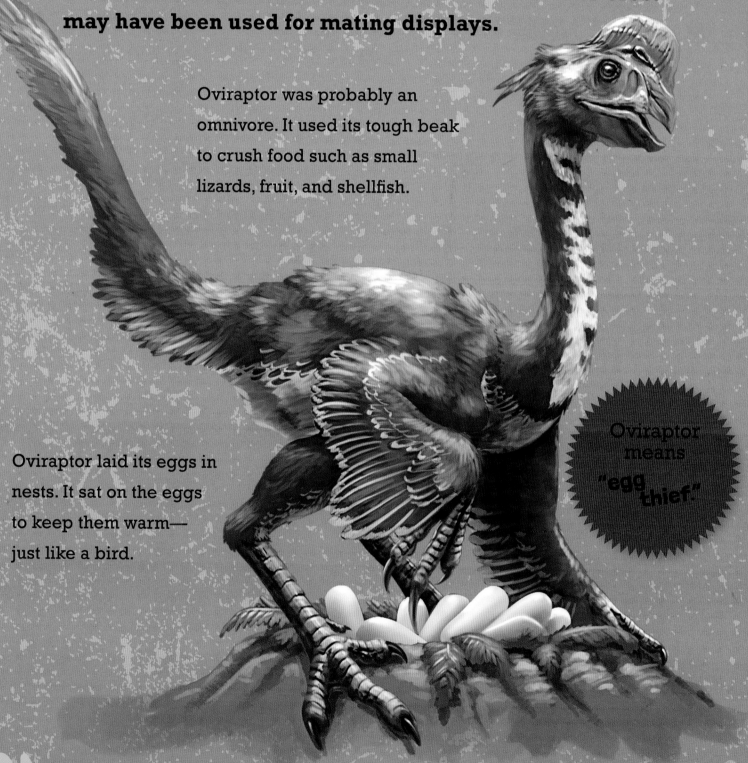

Oviraptor was probably an omnivore. It used its tough beak to crush food such as small lizards, fruit, and shellfish.

Oviraptor laid its eggs in nests. It sat on the eggs to keep them warm— just like a bird.

Oviraptor means "egg thief."

Fast Facts

When: Late Cretaceous period

Food: Meat, eggs, insects, shellfish, and plants

Size: 2 m (6.5 ft) long

You!

Weight: 20–30 kg (44–66 lb)

How it moved: On two legs

Found in: Mongolia, Asia

When the fossilized bones of Oviraptor were found in the nest of Protoceratops, scientists thought that Oviraptor was an egg thief. Now, they think the nest belonged to Oviraptor, and it was actually looking after its own eggs!

Protoceratops

Oviraptor was about the size of an emu.

Features of hunters

Meat-eaters came in many shapes and sizes. However, they all had some things in common—the features that made them dangerous hunters.

Meat-eating dinosaurs had a powerful sense of smell and good eyesight.

They stood on their toes, and their strong legs helped them to catch prey quickly.

Super senses

Legs for running

Carcharodontosaurus
(CAR-kah-roh-don-toh-SORE-us)

Dilophosaurus
(dih-LOW-foh-SORE-us)

The skin or feathers of some hunters were patterned to help them blend into the background. This would have helped these mighty meat-eaters to get close to their prey.

Meat-eating dinosaurs were smarter than plant-eaters. They used their intelligence to hunt down other animals.

Camouflage

Brain power

Tarbosaurus
(TAR-bow-SORE-us)

Chindesaurus
(CHIN-dee-SORE-us)

The terrible claw

Deinonychus (die-NOH-nih-kus) was a light and fast-moving dinosaur. It had a hunting claw on each foot. This meat-eater was one of the smartest dinosaurs around—which made it a deadly predator!

Deinonychus was about 3.4 m (11 ft) long—that's twice as big as Velociraptor. It hunted in packs. It could use its huge claw to kick and tear its prey apart.

Deinonychus' claw was 12 cm (4.7 in) long!

Fast Facts

When: Early Cretaceous period

Food: Plant-eating dinosaurs

Size: 3 m (10 ft) long

You!

Weight: 75 kg (165 lb)

How it moved: On two legs

Found in: USA, North America

This dinosaur may have been covered in feathers to keep it warm. The feathers also may have been used for mating displays!

Deinonychus means "terrible claw."

3. PEACEFUL PLANT-EATERS

About two thirds of dinosaurs were plant-eaters, or herbivores. The biggest herbivores were enormous sauropods. Some sauropods ate enough plants every day to match the weight of a small car!

Brachiosaurus (BRAH-kee-oh-SORE-us) was a sauropod living during the Jurassic period.

Brachiosaurus

Most plant-eaters had blunt teeth for stripping leaves from branches. Some, such as Brachiosaurus, walked on four legs. Others, such as Plateosaurus (PLAH-tee-oh-SORE-us), walked on two.

Fast Facts
Some dinosaurs swallowed rocks (gastroliths) to help break down the plants they'd eaten for lunch!

Blunt teeth

Plateosaurus

Enormous stomach

Plateosaurus was 7 m (22 ft) long.

A huge herbivore

Diplodocus (DIH-ploh-DOH-kus) was HUGE! Its tail was the longest of all the dinosaurs—as long as two tennis courts.

Diplodocus had an enormous appetite. Its peg-shaped teeth could strip the tough leaves from conifers. It also ate leaves from other plants, such as gingkos, ferns, and horsetails.

In 1905, a cast of a Diplodocus skeleton was given to the Natural History Museum in London, UK. Its nickname is "Dippy!"

Diplodocus means "double beam."

Fast Facts

When: Late Jurassic period

Food: Leaves and soft plants

Size:
26 m
(85 ft) long

→ You!

Weight: 25,000 kg (27.5 tons)

How it moved: Slowly, on four legs

Found in: USA, North America

Diplodocus may have used its tail to whip predators!

Spiky protector

Stegosaurus (STEH-goh-SORE-us) was a large, slow-moving plant-eater. It would have defended itself from predators with its powerful spiked tail.

Fast Facts

When: Late Jurassic period

Food: Leaves and plants

Size: 9 m (30 ft) long

You!

Weight: 3,100 kg (3.4 tons)

How it moved: Slowly, on four legs

Found in: Worldwide

Stegosaurus had 17 bony plates on its back. They may have been used to keep the dinosaur cool, or to protect it from meat-eaters. Or they may have been used for impressing possible mates.

This dinosaur had a beak, like a bird. At the back of its mouth were small teeth called "cheek teeth" that it used to chew plant leaves.

Stegosaurus means "roof lizard."

Three-horned threat

Triceratops had three horns on its face. It had a bony plate called a frill at the back of its skull. A predator would have to be pretty fearless to attack this dinosaur!

Triceratops means "three-horned face."

This plant-eater had a large head, about 3 m (10 ft) long. That's a third of its 9-m (30-ft) length! Triceratops had a beak like a parrot's. Its cheek teeth helped it chew food.

Triceratops' frill may have made it look more impressive.

Fast Facts

When: Late Cretaceous period

Food: Leaves and plants

Size: 9 m (30 ft) long

You!

Weight: 5,500 kg (6.1 tons)

How it moved: On four legs

Found in: USA, North America

Triceratops probably charged at its enemy, such as other Triceratops or predators like T. rex. It rushed with its head down and horns forward.

Thick-headed lizard

Pachycephalosaurus (PAH-kee-seh-fah-low-SORE-us) had a thick skull, with a dome-shaped, bony lump on top. It used this tough part of its skull to ram other dinosaurs.

This plant-eater was probably a herd animal. Its thick skull might have been used to defend itself against predators, or in mating displays.

Fast Facts

When: Late Cretaceous period

Food: Plants, fruit, and seeds

Size: 8 m (26 ft) long

You!

Weight: 3,000 kg (3.3 tons)

How it moved: On two legs

Found in: Canada and USA, North America

Pachycephalosaurus means

"thick-headed lizard."

Pachycephalosaurus' skull was up to 25 cm (10 in) thick!

Pachycephalosaurus had bumpy knobs on its snout and around the dome on its head. However, its teeth were very small. It could not have eaten tough plants.

Gentle giants

Sauropods were the biggest animals that ever walked on land. Mamenchisaurus' neck alone was 13 m (42.6 ft) long. Its full height would have reached the top of a building with four floors!

Sauropod means "lizard-footed."

Sauropods were the biggest dinosaurs. It would take a stack of three T. rex to reach the height of Mamenchisaurus!

An adult sauropod would have been too big to attack. Any predator that dared to get close enough would have been swiped by a sauropod's long tail.

Sauropods may have been big, but they had very small heads for their bodies. And they had even smaller brains! Luckily, these gentle giants didn't need to be clever.

Mamenchisaurus

A spiny sauropod

Amargasaurus (ah-MAR-gah-SORE-us) was a migrating dinosaur that moved in herds searching for food. This plant-eater may have eaten leaves whole, without even chewing its food before swallowing!

A bizarre-looking dinosaur, Amargasaurus was smaller and had a shorter neck than most other sauropods. It may have looked for food on the ground, rather than up high.

Fast Facts

When: Early Cretaceous period

Food: Tough plants

Size: 12 m (39 ft) long

← You!

Weight: 9,000 kg (10 tons)

How it moved: On four legs

Found in: Argentina, South America

Amargasaurus had two rows of spines along its back. These spines may have been joined by skin, so they looked like a sail. The "sail" may have been used for protection, in mating displays, or for keeping the dinosaur cool.

Amargasaurus means "Amarga lizard." La Amarga is a place in Argentina.

Safety in numbers

Some plant-eating dinosaurs lived in groups for protection, like zebra do today. They roamed in search of food. Some sauropods may have migrated great distances.

Herding dinosaurs could warn each other of danger. Parasaurolophus (PAH-rah-sore-OH-loh-fus) was especially good at this. It could make a loud noise by pushing air into the hollow crest on top of its head.

Parasaurolophus

Chasmosaurus (KAZ-moh-SORE-us)

Chasmosaurus and Centrosaurus probably lived in large groups. Younger animals did not have horns. They would have been protected by older members of the herd.

Centrosaurus (SEN-troh-SORE-us)

Spiky hands

Iguanodon (ig-WAH-no-don) was a plant-eating dinosaur that could move around on two or four legs. It had a toothless beak and cheek teeth, which it used to chew tough plants.

This plant-eater had a bendy little finger for grasping food, and sharp thumb claws for prying open tough fruits. The claws also protected it against predators.

Fast Facts

When: Early Cretaceous period

Food: Plants

Size: 10 m (33 ft) long

You!

Weight: 4,000 kg (4.4 tons)

How it moved: On two or four legs

Found: Worldwide

Iguanadon means "iguana tooth."

Scientists used to think that Iguanodon's thumb claws were horns!

Iguanodon lived during the Cretaceous period when Pangaea was breaking up into many continents. Fossils of this dinosaur have been found in North America, Europe, and Asia.

A living tank

Ankylosaurus (AN-kuh-loh-SORE-us) was a big, heavy plant-eater that moved slowly. Because of its large size, it needed to eat a lot of plants to stay alive!

Ankylosaurus had short legs, so it walked fairly low to the ground. Its narrow beak and small teeth helped it strip leaves from low-lying plants.

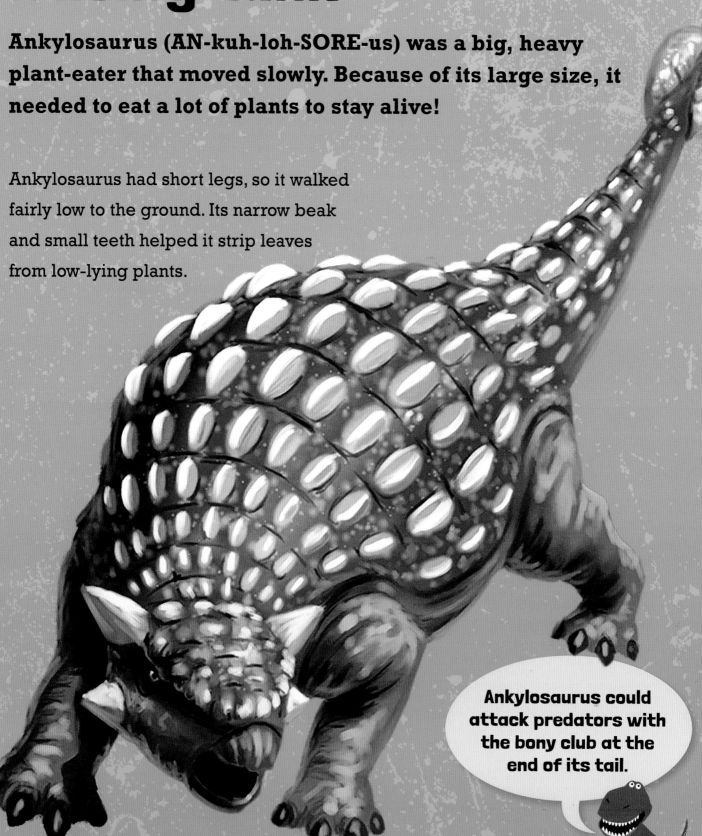

Ankylosaurus could attack predators with the bony club at the end of its tail.

Fast Facts

When: Late Cretaceous period

Food: Plants

Size: 7 m (23 ft) long

← You!

Weight: 4,000–7,000 kg (4.4–7.7 tons)

How it moved: On four legs

Found in: Canada and USA, North America

This dinosaur is possibly the most heavily-protected dinosaur we know about. Its body was covered in thick bony plates, two rows of spikes, large horns, and a tail like a club. Its plates were probably made from keratin—the same stuff as your fingernails!

Ankylosaurus means "stiff lizard."

Dinosaur defenders

Scientists think that many plant-eaters had tough, leathery skin. This was to protect them from the razor-sharp teeth of meat-eating dinosaurs. But many had other weapons they could use in an attack.

Size was a big help! Only ferocious predators or pack hunters would try to kill a mighty sauropod, such as Titanosaurus (TIE-tan-oh-SORE-us). Others, such as Tuojiangosaurus (too-YANG-oh-sore-us) and Styracosaurus (sty-RAH-koh-SORE-us), protected themselves with horns, bony plates, and spikes.

Styracosaurus

Titanosaurus

Camouflage markings may have helped plant-eating dinosaurs blend into their surroundings. This way, hungry predators might not see them.

Tuojiangosaurus

4. T. REX: THE MOST FAMOUS DINOSAUR OF ALL

Tyrannosaurus rex was a truly fearsome dinosaur. It had long, razor-sharp teeth and a powerful bite. Measuring 12 m (39 ft) from tip to tail, it was as long as a bus!

T. rex could be up to 6 m (20 ft) tall. That's more than three times as tall as an adult human.

Compared to its huge body, T. rex's arms were tiny! They were only about 1 m (3 ft) long.

Fast Facts

When: Late Cretaceous period

Food: Other dinosaurs

Size: 12 m (39 ft) long

←You!

Weight: 7,000 kg (7.7 tons)

How it moved: On two legs

Found in: Canada and USA, North America

About 30 Tyrannosaurus rex fossils have been found, but none are complete. Scientists think this prehistoric monster had about 200 bones. However, nobody knows exactly how many.

"T. rex" is short for Tyrannosaurus rex. It means **"tyrant lizard king."**

The world of T. rex

Tyrannosaurus rex roamed the Earth during the Cretaceous period, about 65 million years ago. It lived in a part of the world that is now North America.

At that time, North America was warm and humid. T. rex lived in forests near big rivers. It spent much of its time hunting among the trees.

Fast Facts

The Cretaceous period lasted about 79 million years. It was longer than the Triassic and Jurassic periods.

Many other dinosaurs lived alongside T. rex. It shared its world with other well-known dinosaurs such as Iguanodon, Ankylosaurus, Triceratops, and Maiasaura.

Iguanodon

Ankylosaurus

What did T. rex look like?

T. rex had a huge, heavy head, balanced by a long, stiff tail. Its skull alone was over 1.5 m (5 ft) long. Its tail made up about half the length of its body.

T. rex was built for running quickly after its prey. Its powerful legs ended with claws that could hold down prey. Its sharp teeth were the perfect weapons to tear into flesh!

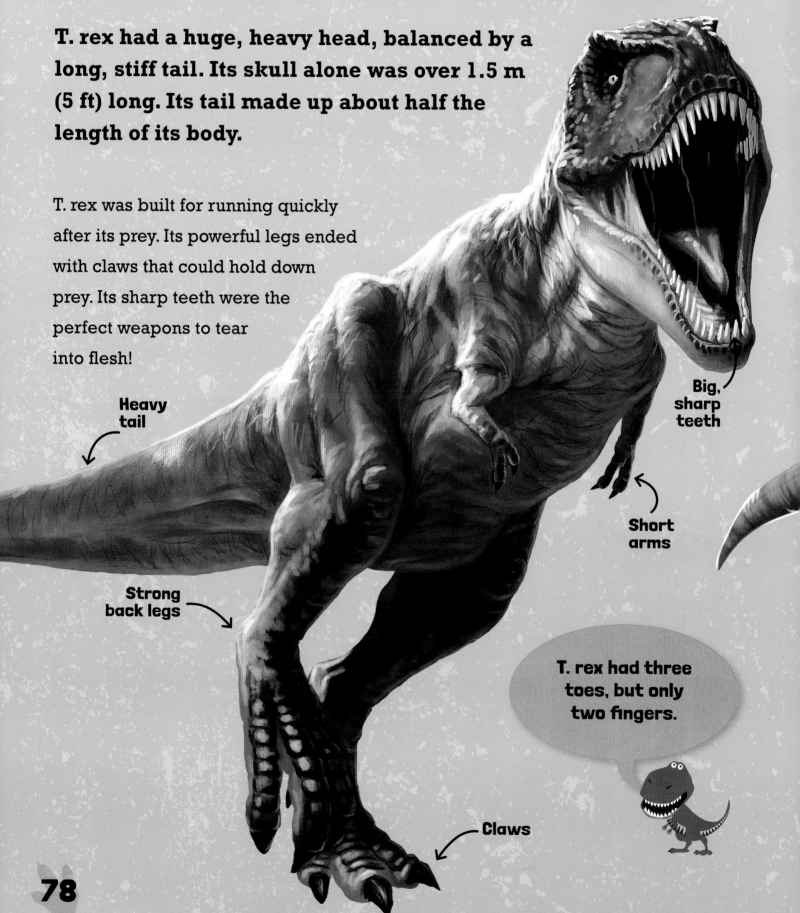

Heavy tail

Big, sharp teeth

Short arms

Strong back legs

T. rex had three toes, but only two fingers.

Claws

Fast Facts

The eyeball of a T. rex was the size of a human adult's fist!

Was this mighty meat-eater brown, green, or red? Was it striped or spotted? Unless a fossil of T. rex's skin is found, we will never know for sure. Some scientists even think that T. rex had feathers!

A T. rex with feathers might have looked like this.

Tremendous teeth

Tyrannosaurus rex's jaws contained 60 sharp teeth. Each tooth was as long as a human hand! Its bite was three times more powerful than a lion's. No other land animal has ever bitten that hard.

T. rex's jaws were 1.2 m (4 ft) long! That's the size of a 7-year-old child...

T. rex could hack away huge chunks of meat and crush bones as it ate. It could easily tear off 230 kg (500 lb) of flesh in a single bite. That's the weight of a large pig.

Fast Facts

When one of T. rex's teeth broke, a new one simply grew in its place.

With its long skull and wide jaws, T. rex may even have swallowed small dinosaurs whole!

Hunter or scavenger?

Some scientists think that Tyrannosaurus rex hunted and killed most of the meat that it ate, like a lion. Others think that it mostly scavenged dead or dying dinosaurs, like a hyena.

T. rex used its good sense of smell to find food. It may have driven other predators away from their meals. They would have been scared away by the size of this mighty dinosaur.

From fossil finds, we know that T. rex ate horned dinosaurs, such as Triceratops, and duck-billed dinosaurs, such as Maiasaura.

Triceratops

Maiasaura lived in large herds. T. rex probably picked off old or sick animals.

Maiasaura

Fast Facts

When food was scarce, T. rex would turn on each other! T. rex bones have been found in the stomachs of other T. rex.

A fierce fighter

T. rex probably hunted alone. Its size meant that T. rex was big enough to take on large dinosaurs. It may have even attacked huge sauropods, such as Alamosaurus (AH-lah-moh-SORE-us)!

Alamosaurus

Fast Facts

T. rex was one of the dinosaurs that inspired the movie character, Godzilla!

We know from fossils that Tyrannosaurus rex sometimes lived together. However, we also know that these enormous reptiles often fought each other.

Many Tyrannosaurus rex skeletons have bite marks from the teeth of other T. rex. They probably fought over food, territory, or mates.

The most famous T. rex fossil, "Sue," has bite marks on her face from another T. rex.

Young T. rex

T. rex started out as an egg, which hatched into a baby dinosaur. No fossils of T. rex eggs have ever been found, so we don't know what exact size or shape they would have been.

Young T. rex grew quickly. By the age of 14 it weighed as much as a baby elephant.

2 years old   **14 years old**   **25 years old**

It's possible a mother T. rex stayed with its young when they were small and vulnerable to attack. T. rex mothers probably taught their young how to hunt. As they grew up, they would start hunting on their own.

Young T. rex

Young T. rex

Mother T. rex

How do we know about Tyrannosaurus rex?

By looking at fossils, scientists can learn about T. rex's body, the way it lived, and the world around it.

The first T. rex fossil was discovered in 1902 by a famous fossil hunter called Barnum Brown. He dug it up it in Montana, USA. Since then, T. rex fossils have been found in Canada, the USA, and Mongolia.

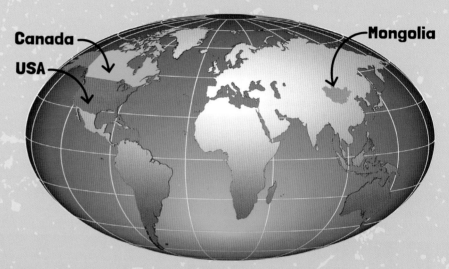

Canada

USA

Mongolia

You can see T. rex skeletons at many natural history museums.

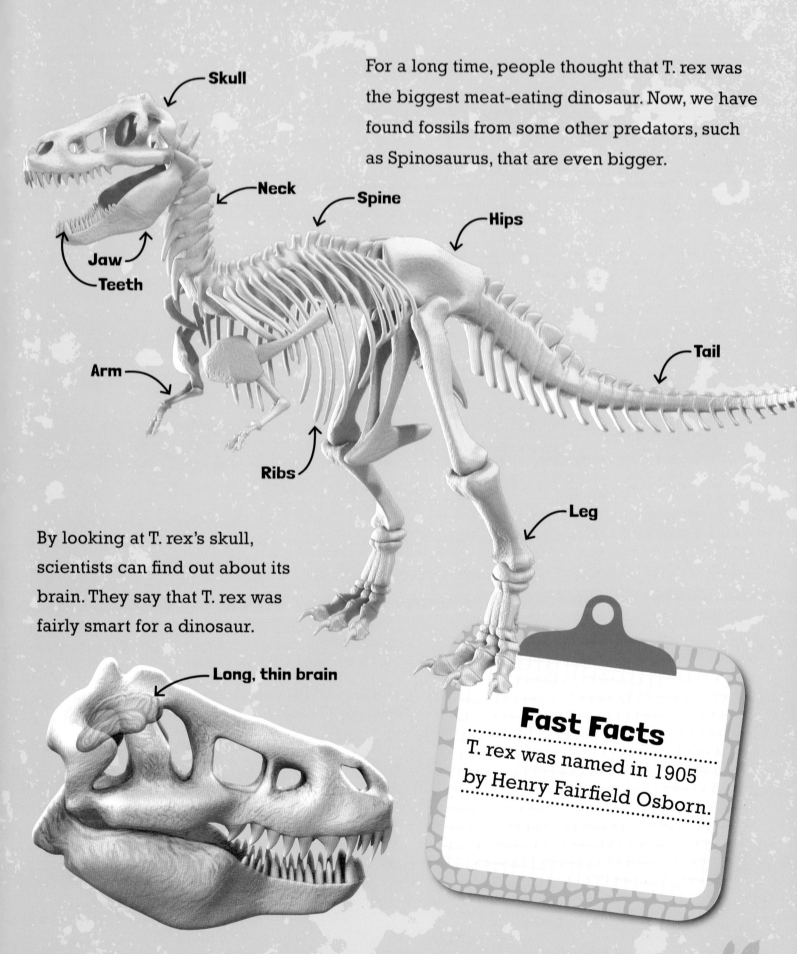

Skull

Neck

Spine

Hips

Jaw

Teeth

Arm

Ribs

Tail

Leg

For a long time, people thought that T. rex was the biggest meat-eating dinosaur. Now, we have found fossils from some other predators, such as Spinosaurus, that are even bigger.

By looking at T. rex's skull, scientists can find out about its brain. They say that T. rex was fairly smart for a dinosaur.

Long, thin brain

Fast Facts

T. rex was named in 1905 by Henry Fairfield Osborn.

Famous fossils

Many T. rex fossils have been given nicknames. The largest fossil is called "Sue." She is 12 m (42 ft) long and 3.6 m (12 ft) high.

In 2001, the most complete T. rex fossil was found. The bones belonged to a juvenile T. rex, nicknamed "Jane." At 6 m (21 ft), she is just half the length of Sue.

"Sue"

"Jane"

Fast Facts

Sue is named after Sue Hendrickson, the paleontologist who discovered her in 1990.

Sue would have been really fearsome, even for a T. rex! From looking at her fossil, scientists can tell that she had been in a lot of fights. Sue was about 28 years old when she died. She is the oldest Tyrannosaurus rex that we know about.

Might Sue have looked like this?

Sue was sold to a museum in the United States for $8 million!

Myths about T. rex

There are a lot of tall tales about T. rex! The truth might surprise you.

T. rex lived during the Jurassic period.

False! In fact, it lived millions of years later, during the late Cretaceous period.

T. rex was the biggest meat-eating dinosaur.

False! T. rex was a top predator, but it wasn't the biggest meat-eating dinosaur that ever lived.

T. rex could run as fast as a car!

False! It's unlikely that T. rex could run at 48 km (30 mi) per hour. It was more like 19–29 km (12–18 mi) per hour.

T. rex was green.

Maybe! We don't know what its skin looked like.

T. rex was smart!

False! It was smarter than its prey ... but most dinosaurs were not very intelligent.

T. rex could only see you if you moved.

False! T. rex had great eyesight. It would have spotted you, even standing still!

Glossary

adapt Change to new conditions.

ankylosaurids Plant-eating dinosaurs with beaks and club tails.

archosaurs The group of reptiles that dinosaurs are descended from.

camouflage An animal's look that helps it blend in with its surroundings.

carnivore An animal that feeds on other animals.

ceratopsians Plant-eating dinosaurs with horns and frills.

cheek teeth Small teeth at the back of the mouth used for chewing.

climate The weather conditions of a particular area.

crest A comb, tuft of feathers, fur, or skin on the head of an animal.

Cretaceous period A period in Earth's history, between 144 and 65 million years ago.

extinct No longer living.

fossil The remains of an animal or plant, preserved for millions of years.

frill A fringe of feathers or hair.

gastrolith A small stone swallowed by a dinosaur to help digest its food.

herbivore An animal that eats plants.

herd A large group of animals.

Jurassic period A time in Earth's history, between 206 to 144 million years ago.

juvenile A young or baby animal.

mammal A warm-blooded animal.

mate The partner of an animal.

mating display Things animals do to attract a mate.

meteorite A piece of rock that has fallen to Earth from space.

migrate To move from one area to another, usually in search of food.

omnivore An animal that eats plants and meat.

Pangaea A prehistoric supercontinent made up of all the continents found in the modern world.

plunder To steal.

predator An animal that eats other animals.

prehistoric From a time before written records.

prey An animal that is eaten by other animals.

pterosaur A winged reptile that could fly.

reptile A cold-blooded creature with dry, scaly skin.

saliva The watery liquid produced in the mouth to help chewing and swallowing.

sauropods Large, plant-eating dinosaurs.

scavenge To search for and collect.

serrated Having a jagged edge like a saw.

territory An area of land that an animal lives within and defends.

theropods Meat-eating dinosaurs.

Triassic period A period in Earth's history, between 248 and 206 million years ago.

vulnerable Exposed to the possibility of attack.

Index